# The
# Women's
# Land Army

### BOB POWELL &
### NIGEL WESTACOTT

Cover photographs:*front*: Trainee Land Girls
hoeing mangolds at the East Sussex School of
Agriculture, Plumpton; *back*: A hoeing gang
enjoying a break while working on potatoes on
War Agricultural Committee land on the South
Downs at Saltdean, 1948.

Title page: Eileen Mitchell (née Vile) is on the
binder, with her sister Iris driving the Fordson
tractor at Lower Hill Farm, Pulborough, Sussex,
1945. In fact they have changed seats for the
photograph, because Eileen normally drove. The
two sisters had a third sister, Winifred, who was
also in the Land Army but worked elsewhere.

First published in 1997
Reprinted 1998, 1999 (twice), 2000

This edition first published in 2009

The History Press
The Mill, Brimscombe Port
Stroud, Gloucestershire, GL5 2QG
www.thehistorypress.co.uk

British Library Cataloguing in Publication Data.
A catalogue record for this book is available from the British Library.

ISBN 978 0 7524 5116 9

Typesetting and origination by The History Press
Printed in Great Britain

# CONTENTS

A Harvest Festival Land Army Parade in Chichester, West Sussex, 16 November 1945.

# INTRODUCTION

The roots of the Women's Land Army lie in the First World War. It has to be borne in mind that in 1914 50 per cent of the food needed by Britain's population of 36 million was imported. By 1915 the enemy's navy had begun to mount a successful blockade of our ports, and the question of a food shortage was already causing concern to Lord Selbourne, the Minister for Agriculture. However, the Prime Minister, H.H. Asquith, said in July of that year that, in his opinion there was not 'the least fear of any probable or conceivable development . . . that can be a serious menace to our food supply' [*sic*].

The labour shortage created by the taking of farm and other workers for military service resulted in the Government announcing its intention, in 1915, to compile a 'Register of Women: willing to do industrial, agricultural and clerical work'. However, little happened after months of talk between numerous official bodies, until Lord Selbourne appointed Miss Meriel Talbot (later Dame Meriel Talbot DBE) as adviser to the Minister.

In December 1916 the new Prime Minister, David Lloyd George, granted backing for a new Food Production Department, among whose seven divisions were included 'Labour' and 'Women'.

1917 was a gloom-ridden year. There was a near desperate situation on the farms, caused by the lack of labour, and indeed of horses commandeered by the military, coupled with a predicted disastrous harvest. This was compounded by the success of the enemy U-boat submarines in devastating our ships importing food. It was calculated that the country's reserves of food barely exceeded three weeks. It was then that the Women's Land Army was born.

Recruits were offered the chance to serve in one of three sections: Agriculture, Timber Cutting or Forage (animal feed-stuffs). All were under the new Food Production Department, with Sir Arthur Lee as Director. The women's branch of this department, with Miss Talbot as Director, was also responsible for guiding and nurturing the Women's Institute, then in its infancy. It was through the Women's Institute connection that Miss Talbot was able to recruit Lady Trudie Denman to become involved with the Women's Land Army, as Honorary Assistant Director.

A poster used to recruit Land Girls during the First World War, 1914–18. (reproduced by permission of the Imperial War Museum)

The organization now went ahead at express speed, and a measure of its success can be gauged by unofficial figures recorded in 1918, that 23,000 Land Girls had been at work. This was the number accepted from 45,000 applicants. To quote from a letter written by Miss Talbot to *The Times* in 1941: 'The returns (from a survey taken in 1918 of 12,637 Land Army members) showed that work was distributed as follows: 5,734 milkers: 293 tractor drivers: 3,971 field workers: 635 carters: 260 ploughmen: 84 thatchers: 21 shepherds' [*sic*]. The First World War Women's Land Army was finally disbanded in 1919.

The work and experiences of these early Land Girls has been recorded in print, but there are very few surviving photographs taken by or of the girls themselves; the day of the Box Brownie for all had not yet arrived.

Before the Second World War things began to get organized in 1938 for another Women's Land Army. Volunteers were registered, and Lady Denman accepted the post of Honorary Director. With her experiences from the First World War, she had no hesitation in insisting that the entire organization regarding recruitment, enlisting, placement and welfare of the Land Girls must be in the hands of a single body, staffed by women. By June 1938 she had selected the chairmen of the county committees in readiness for the outbreak of war.

In February 1939 Lady Denman offered the use of her own home at Balcombe Place, Sussex, as the headquarters of the Women's Land Army. On 1 June 1939 the second Women's Land Army was officially formed. The headquarters staff moved to Balcombe Place on 29 August 1939, just days before war was declared. Recruitment offices opened all over the country in towns and cities, one even being situated in London's Oxford Street.

There were strong appeals on radio and in the newspapers, and Lady Denman herself was very active in vocal persuasion. It was said that her invitations to stay as a guest in friends' houses while touring the country were severely curtailed when her hostesses found that some of their few remaining servants left to join the Land Army within days of her visit!

The primary reason to join the WLA was patriotism, but the girls responded to the call for an unlimited variety of reasons: a wish to avoid marching as in the women's military services, a healthy country life, not having to work in munitions factories, to get away from home or a job 'in service', and even 'anything for a laugh'.

The girls were first interviewed at the recruitment offices, to see if they were suitable, then enrolled. The official minimum age to join was 17½, but it seemed to be quite usual for girls of 17 to be accepted. Indeed, numerous girls aged 16 were accepted, if they lied about their age and looked big and strong! The medical examination given varied enormously, and one girl said that having stated she didn't suffer from flat feet or varicose veins she was accepted without further examination!

The recruits were notified when and where to report for training, or in the early days of the war went straight to work. Uniforms were usually sent to their homes (numerous dress rehearsals in front of the mirror and family, and for many girls a trip down to the local photographer), or sometimes the new recruit had to await their arrival where she had to report. At this point the lives of many girls changed abruptly as they left home for the first time, not always going to ideal working and living conditions.

In 1994 an appeal was made for photographs and memorabilia of the Women's Land Army by the Weald & Downland Open Air Museum at Singleton, West Sussex. The aim was to stage an exhibition in tribute to the Women's Land Army. However, it was soon realized what an enormous store of agricultural history was in the hands of these ex-Land Girls. Following an overwhelming response a vast treasure house of photographs was produced by the 'girls', mostly taken with their own cameras, which reflected not only their work but the British countryside at that time.

Once the exhibition was opened, with a gathering of over fifty ex-Land Girls who had given assistance, very many more of the 'girls' came to visit. Many brought even more photographs, of what a number termed 'some of the happiest days of our lives'.

It seemed a duty to make certain that a good selection of the photographs, once brought to light, should remain as a permanent record and be available to all those interested.

A First World War photographic postcard of Land Girls in the official uniform posing with working horses. The back of the postcard was inscribed: 'Love to Ethel, + is myself. Others our girls.'

# UNIFORM

*Baggy Brown Brown Breeches And A Cowboy Hat* was the title of one Land Girl's book containing her reminiscences. Despite this description the 'Walking Out' uniform could be very smart, even if some of it had to be 'home tailored', and the hat bent to suit the personality of the wearer!

Laced brown brogue shoes were worn with brown corduroy (or occasionally gabardine) breeches, and fawn knee-length woollen socks. A smart green V-necked long-sleeved ribbed pullover was worn over a fawn short-sleeved Aertex shirt, with the WLA tie added for formal wear. The uniform was topped with the brown felt 'pork-pie'-style hat, with the WLA badge on the band. This uniform was completed by a good quality melton three-quarter length brown overcoat that was both warm and rainproof (at least until it got wet right through!). For parades and rallies the WLA armband was also worn on the left arm. The colour reflected each five years of service, and apart from the WLA and a crown woven into the cloth, the girls sewed on half diamond cloth badges for each six months of service.

The working uniform of brown dungarees with matching jacket had to serve for most of the work. Wellington boots were issued when available, and some girls received leather ankle boots. Extremes of hot, cold and inclement weather led to many unofficial variations of the uniform. The range varied from the adaptation of dungarees into shorts (some were very short!) during the hot summers, to outer layers of old sacks tied round with binder twine during the worst of the winter rain.

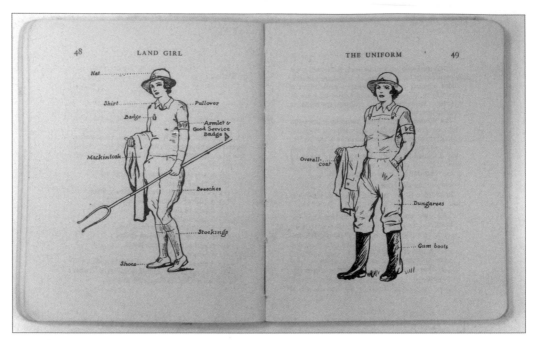

The official uniform as issued to most Land Girls, 1939–50. This illustration is from *Land Girl*, by W.E. Shewell-Cooper, a manual for volunteers published in 1941, price 1*s*.

Miss Margery Kent poses for a photograph in her 'best' uniform shortly after it was issued. The photo was taken at Sutton in Surrey, 28 December 1942.

A party of Land Girls wear their best uniform on a visit to Maidstone Zoo in 1943. The day out was organized by the local officer for girls working in the area. Pat Ware (née Taylor), on the right wearing a hat, worked for Mr John Berridge, a Covent Garden Market stallholder who grew vegetables for sale in London on land requisitioned by the Kent War Agriculture Executive Committee.

Betty Merrett (née Long) wears gum boots with her uniform for tractor driving, 1944. The tractor is a Fordson Standard model 'N'. The boots were often in short supply owing to the wartime restriction on rubber.

# Look Smart in
# HEBDEN BREECHES

## Perfect TO-MEASURE FIT
## UNBEATABLE   VALUE !

The Hebden Cord Co., famous throughout the land for their postal bargains in Ladies' Breeches, make this Special Offer to members of the Women's Land Army. For the remarkably low figure of only 12/6 post free we will tailor you a pair of hard-wearing breeches strictly to your measurements. Perfect fit guaranteed, while our direct-selling methods ensure unequalled value. Send NOW, and get back to the land smartly.

FROM
## 12/6
**DRILL COATS**
from 11/6
POST FREE
*(including Pur chase Tax).*

### TO MAKE
### ORDERING EASY

We will send you Free Patterns of Velvet Cords, Bedfords, Whip-cords, Saddle Tweeds, Cavalry Tweeds, etc., also Style Book and Self-Measurement Chart. SEND NOW to:

# HEBDEN CORD Co.
## (Dept. L.G.)
# HEBDEN BRIDGE, Yorks.
*Telephone : 189*

*The Land Girl* magazine, published monthly, carried this advertisement in many of its issues. This example dates from February 1941. Those who could afford them were able to order more flatteringly cut breeches than the official baggy versions.

A group of market gardening Land Girls at Manor Fruit Farm, near Normandy in Surrey, showing the issued working overalls. The girls called them dungarees. The addition of the leather belt was adopted by most but not all girls. Left to right: Doreen Puttock, Iris Mais, Marjorie ?, Ruth Lamdin, Kathleen Reigate, Renée Middleton (née Abbott).

'Mollie and Beryl' show the working uniform, with and without the overall jacket. Mollie Sivyer is on the left.

Eileen Mitchell (née Vile) is ready for work accompanied by her junior assistant Joan Geall (the farmer's daughter) at Lower Hill Farm, Pulborough, Sussex, 14 April 1945. The little girl's uniform had been made by her older sister from one of Eileen's worn-out overalls. The hat was genuine and Eileen's.

Hot weather produced quick alterations to the overalls. The ground must still have been muddy as shown by their wearing turned-down gum boots, but the chorus line looks very happy in spite of it. This was a hoeing gang from the hostel at Dyke Road, Brighton, enjoying a break while working on potatoes on War Agricultural Committee land on the South Downs at Saltdean, 1948. Jean Stemp (née Ellis), known as 'Ginger', is second from the right.

*TWO*

# HOSTELS & BILLETS

Many of the Land Girls were placed in lodgings and billets near their place of work. These could be cottages in an adjacent village, with the families of fellow farm workers, or living in the farmhouse with the farmer and his wife. Many billets were pleasant, but some varied from poor to atrocious.

Few of the cottages boasted baths or readily available hot water for washing, and the bedding provided was none too clean. A few landladies took rations intended for the Land Girls to add to the meals of their own families, giving the girls small portions and the poorer quality food. Occasionally girls living-in with the farmer and his family were treated as though they were household servants as well as farm workers.

A good and efficient Land Army local representative with the welfare of her girls at heart could often sort out these difficulties by a word in the right place, or moving a girl to another billet. However, it was not unknown for the local representative to be on familiar terms with the farmer or cottager in her area, and so to take their part in disputes.

When the girls settled down and found their feet they could often find alternative billets for themselves. Nevertheless, the feelings of these young girls, often moving from home in towns and cities for the first time in their lives, and being pitched into this rural environment, can be imagined.

As the numbers of Land Girls increased and mobile gangs were formed for labour-intensive work, hostels were opened to accommodate girls in available vacant country houses and schools. The numbers accommodated at each hostel could be as low as six, or up to a hundred girls. Once the initial problems were overcome most provided an acceptable standard of food and accommodation, but the comfort of a hostel depended on the attitude of the resident warden and her staff. Many wardens were like mothers to their girls, but some were too strict or too indifferent; one was found to be selling the girls' rations on the black market!

Doreen Peskett (née Strange) found she had to share a bed with her landlady, Mrs Walder, at her first billet. The tiny cottage was at Plummer's Plain, near Horsham in Sussex.

Doreen Peskett later moved to a billet with farmers Ted and Freda Cox, and their sons Michael (left) and Christopher (right). Doreen (on the right) shared this billet with Muriel Bushby (née Merrett), on the left, at Warnham Court Farm, Horsham, Sussex.

Phyllis Dudgeon (right) spent her entire WLA service, 1941–50, living in the farmhouse with Mr and Mrs Bidewell at Newhouse Farm, Shillinglee, near Chiddingfold, Surrey. (Mrs Bidewell is on the left wearing overalls and also included in the photo are the Bidewells' three nieces). Phyllis did her milking training at the farm, then stayed on. When the WLA disbanded in 1950 she continued until the farmer retired in December 1959 – a total of eighteen years at the one farm.

The Women's Land Army hostel at Northlands, near Chichester. Phyllis Dudgeon appears in the back row, just to the left of the door pillar.

Another photo of the Northlands hostel, on the occasion of a visit by Lady Trudie Denman (Honorary Director of the Women's Land Army). Lady Denman appears to be dressed to go on to some more formal function. The face of the very popular West Sussex WLA County Secretary, Miss Forbes-Adams, can be seen at the rear, to the right of Lady Denman.

The other face of hostels: Nissen huts at Bishop's Wood, Shropshire, June 1943. Back row, left to right: Paddy Hunt, Miss Johnson (staff), Daphne Bland, Miss Davis (staff), Janet Golding. Middle row: Thes Warren, Doreen Bramley, Joan Smith, Eve Groman. Front row: Ann Stehenberg, Nora Ellam, Vicky ?, Dorothy Johnson, Lily Dane. The photograph was taken by Hilda Pearson (née Roylands).

A photograph first published in *The Land Girl* magazine of recruits at Pawston Hostel in Northumberland, February 1941.

Another kind of hostel: Rest Break House at Torquay, Devon. Girls went here to convalesce after illness or injury. This photograph was produced by Inez Kensett (née Rapley) who enjoyed one of its rarely available holidays for the longer-serving girls.

# THREE

# TRAINING

During the early part of the Second World War training of the girls took place at designated training farms, for short periods, or was just training on the job at the place of work.

As things became more organized periods of training, usually of six weeks, took place at existing agricultural colleges. Colleges used in the south of England included Brinsbury College at Pulborough, Plumpton Agricultural College and Sparsholt Farm Institute near Winchester. During the first years Land Girls were given training in hand- and machine-milking, animal husbandry, tractor driving and handwork jobs. Later more specialized courses such as thatching, hedge laying and pest control were available.

As the increasing need for more and more food production became apparent, and more tractors were available to farmers, there was an immediate need for extra Land Girl tractor drivers. Specialist tractor driver training units were set up, such as the one established on Brighton Racecourse, under the umbrella of the East Sussex War Agricultural Executive Committee and Brighton Corporation.

Some girls retain bitter memories of early training farms, where they were regarded as little more than free labour, being taught no more than how to fork muck into a wheelbarrow and wash down the cow stalls. Fortunately this sort of thing was soon rooted out, and most girls found training alongside other novices hard work, but endurable.

Over the ten-year period Land Girls discovered some very valuable talents and developed great skills. Many employers gave glowing reports of their girls; for example, 'my girls are as good as any male farm worker, and often much more conscientious.'

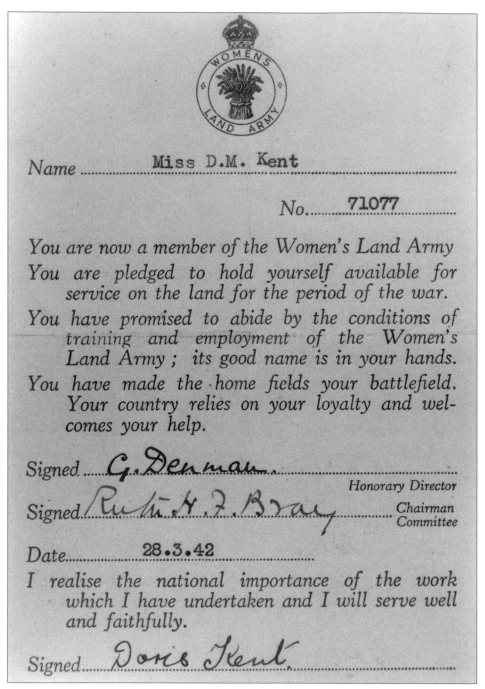

Name ..... **Miss D.M. Kent** .....

No. ..... **71077** .....

*You are now a member of the Women's Land Army*

*You are pledged to hold yourself available for service on the land for the period of the war.*

*You have promised to abide by the conditions of training and employment of the Women's Land Army ; its good name is in your hands.*

*You have made the home fields your battlefield. Your country relies on your loyalty and welcomes your help.*

Signed ..... *G. Denman* .....
                                          Honorary Director

Signed ..... *Ruth H.F. Bray* .....
                                          Chairman
                                          Committee

Date ..... **28.3.42** .....

*I realise the national importance of the work which I have undertaken and I will serve well and faithfully.*

Signed ..... *Doris Kent* .....

Doris Kent's WLA Joining Certificate, which is signed by Lady Trudie Denman as Honorary Director of the Women's Land Army. The girl's signature binds her to a very strong commitment for the duration of the war. The reverse side states: 'The Undertaking which every volunteer signs on being accepted as a member of the Women's Land Army allows her to apply to her County Secretary for permission to resign if circumstances arise which make it difficult for her to keep her promise of service. She must not resign until this permission is received and when it is received she must return her uniform and badge to the County Land Army office.'

A group of trainee Land Girls who were sent for four weeks training at the East Sussex School of Agriculture, Plumpton, near Lewes in Sussex. The school trained Land Girls from 1939 to 1944.

A new WLA intake at the East Sussex School of Agriculture, all displaying their identification labels. Second from the left is Mr Sansom (farm bailiff). Fourth from the right is Mr Richard H.B. Jesse (College Principal). On the extreme right is Lady Diana De La War (East Sussex County Organizer).

Land Girls trainees' dining room at East Sussex School of Agriculture. Connie Edwards (née Caldbeck) is the laughing girl in front of the men in white coats.

Land Girl trainees at Bangor College Farm, Aber, North Wales. The girls were billeted at Aber Falls Halt Hotel during their six weeks of training. Sylvia Baylis (née Rees) is seated on the right, on the sacks.

Two of the first five trainees at the East Sussex School of Agriculture having tractor instruction, July 1939. On the left is Mrs Baker ('Rufus') and on the right is Rosemary Pierce ('Squibs'). The other three initial trainees were Helen Beard (née Coward), Mrs Daft and Kally Sproulle. The instructor, Bill Brown, can be seen behind.

Land Girls under instruction as tractor drivers at the Plumpton School, 1942. Doris Kent is on the extreme right at the back of the Fordson Standard model 'N' tractor. Helen Beard is leaning on the bonnet.

Plumpton School Land Girls being taught how to maintain a binder – a Deering shipped from America. We hope the instructor chastised the girl kneeling on the bed of the binder, a part easily twisted out of shape by actions such as this!

Again at Plumpton, Land Girls are being instructed in driving a pair of Shire horses hitched to a zig-zag harrow. The instructor, Herbert Durrant, looks ready to take over in event of trouble, but the slack reins tend to indicate a fairly placid pair of horses. The girl driving is Joan Scott.

Land Girls posted to the Cowdray Estate at Midhurst, Sussex, were sent for the day to Petersfield Agriculture Show 'to learn what they could about farming and horses'. Betsy Sinclair (née Riddell) is in the centre holding a yearling horse. The photograph dates from 1939.

Land Girl students at an Agriculture Certificate Course held in Cambridgeshire for girls wishing to continue in farming after leaving the Women's Land Army, 1946. The seven-week course was held at Newton Hall Training Centre by the Cambridgeshire War Agriculture Executive Committee and often used local farms. Gladys Pyman was awarded a Certificate in General Agriculture on this course, and went on to manage a Dairy Shorthorn herd on her own. On 3 November 1947 she earned a Certificate of Merit in a Clean Milk Competition held by Cambridge WAEC.

Students on the WLA Agriculture Certificate Course in Cambridgeshire receiving a lecture on dairy hygiene at a local farm.

Another view of the Cambridgeshire WLA Agriculture Certificate Course, where Gladys Pyman and fellow students studied pigs at a farm. This is a pure-bred Wessex Saddleback sow with an excellent litter of piglets.

Connie Edwards (née Caldbeck) while training at Plumpton Agricultural College, 1940. Mrs Edwards was one of six Caldbeck sisters sent by their father from Kilkenny in Ireland to England to help with the war effort by joining the Women's Land Army. She served from 18 September 1939 to 10 September 1949, and (with two of her sisters) married and settled in England.

Land Girls under training as thatchers by the Surrey WAEC at Clandon near Guildford, 1943.

At tea time: Surrey WAEC Land Girl thatching trainees at Clandon, 1943. The girl on the left is Edna Mitchell. Second from the left is Kitty Brunton (née Chandler).

Betty Merrett (née Long), on the right, being shown how to bait a rat trap. She was trained to be a Pest Controller in 1943.

Marjorie Pither describes her first two weeks of service as 'so-called training'. In June 1942 she was sent with twelve other Land Girls to join a gang of casual women field workers from Brighton to cut cabbage and marrows on land being used for vegetable production on Brighton Racecourse. The trainee Land Girls joined the women at Brighton Market each day and were transported by lorry to the work. This photograph was taken when the WVS mobile tea van called during the day. The most notable thing that Marjorie and her colleagues learned during the fortnight seems to have been colourful language!

We think this photograph shows two girls being tested for their Proficiency Certificate, probably in 'General Farm Work', as they are building a load of straw on a cart. The photograph was produced by Inez Kensett (née Rapley), but date and location are unknown.

*F O U R*

# HANDWORK

Girls have always excelled at the delicate handwork required in nurseries and glasshouses, dealing with plants and seedlings. Many girls were drafted in to work in this way to boost production of much-needed vegetables and salad crops. However, many more girls were recruited into the mobile gangs that worked in all weathers, hoeing and singling plants for weeks on end in the open fields. They will all remember how their backs felt in the first few days, but also how they got used to it in the end.

The girls had to cope with all the work done by the men now in the armed forces, and this included all the hard dirty work like muck-spreading by hand, and cold freezing work in the cabbage fields in winter.

As the German blockade of our merchant ships bit harder, so the girls had to take on the extra work now needed to make up for the food that could no longer be imported. That they coped was in itself an enormous tribute to their work. The varied jobs that were done, and done well, are now difficult for them to believe looking back. So many different jobs were tackled as they arose day by day, but probably hoeing and muck-spreading by hand will be most remembered by those who just got on with the job!

Newhouse Farm, Shillinglee, near Chiddingfold, Surrey. Phyllis Dudgeon, right, and Joan are spreading dung by hand from a trailer. This was very hard work, but these girls are smiling.

June 1940. Two of the six Caldbeck sisters over from Kilkenny, Ireland, to join the Women's Land Army, busy hoeing at Earlye Farm, Wadhurst, East Sussex. Pearl (the eldest) is on the right and Ruby is on the left. The third girl is the late Lola Cotton. The other Caldbeck sisters were Connie, Christobel, Joy and Rose (the youngest).

Trainee Land Girls hoeing mangolds at the East Sussex School of Agriculture, Plumpton. The girl on the left, always known as Jim, is Lavender Herbert, the daughter of A.P. Herbert.

'Day' Sparrow works in the cold frames at Plant Protection Ltd, Fernhurst, West Sussex, *c.* 1947.

Land Girls cutting cress in the greenhouses at F. & G. Mizzen Ltd, Bonseys Farm, Woking, *c.* 1944.

Trainee Land Girls working on tomato plants in the horticultural section of the East Sussex School of Agriculture.

F. & G. Mizzen Ltd, Bonseys Farm, Woking, Surrey, c. 1944. Land Girls from a gang are using short-handled hand hoes on carrots. Back row, left to right: Joan Lloyd, Pamela Pleasance, Doris Kent, Mary Shibley, -?-. Middle: -?-. Front row: 'Enid', Joy Deans (née Snow), Kathleen Warren, -?-.

Mollie Sivyer (née Cook) picking tomatoes at Mr Beale's farm, Ferring-on-Sea, Sussex, 1943.

Loading tomatoes at Mr A.W. Milton's Manor Fruit Farm, Normandy, Guildford, Surrey, 1943. Renée Middleton (née Abbott) is on the left of the group.

Picking beans before breakfast on Col. House's market garden at Lee-on-Solent, Hampshire. Daphne Turner (née Hudson) is on the left.

'Joyce and Phyl' picking peas at Mr Beale's farm, Ferring-on-Sea, Sussex, 1943.

Pulling carrots at Ferring-on-Sea. Left to right: 'Phyl', 'Joyce', 'Beryl' and Mollie Sivyer (née Cook). Mollie later worked at a market garden where the owner was found to be growing too high a percentage of flowers compared to vegetables, and his fourteen Land Girls were taken away.

Renée Middleton (née Abbott), on the right, and a fellow Land Girl pick up potatoes at Manor Fruit Farm, Normandy, Surrey, 1941.

Daphne Turner (née Hudson), on the right, filling and loading bags of cabbage at Col. House's market garden at Lee-on-Solent, Hampshire.

Joan Scott picking pears at the East Sussex School of Agriculture, Plumpton. She continued working at the school after training.

Girls from a Surrey WAEC gang based at Burchett's Farm, Stoke, near Guildford, are in nearby orchards pruning fruit trees, 1943. Kitty Brunton (née Chandler) is up a ladder on the left.

At the end of the day: girls being taken back to their hostel by lorry from Col. House's market garden at Lee-on-Solent, Hampshire.

# TRACTOR WORK

With the able-bodied younger farm workers gone to war, and the introduction of tractors to what had previously been horse-only farms, a trained Land Girl often became the farm's only expert tractor machinery operator.

Girls were given intensive training at the special schools, such as the one on Brighton Racecourse. They left these schools with a fairly sound knowledge of how to drive and maintain their tractor, how to plough and how to operate a number of implements. Some of the girls were given training on the job at the farms where they worked.

It was during the period of vastly increased food production that many small farms saw their first tractor arrive, often on hire or loan from the county War Agricultural Executive Committee (generally known as the 'War Ag').

The idea of girls operating new modern machinery like tractors was quite revolutionary, and newsworthy. The combination of new machinery and girls doing a man's job attracted the reporter and photographer.

*Joan Tilly and Ruth Lamdin with a model 'F' Fordson tractor at Manor Fruit Farm, Normandy, Surrey, 1941.*

Sybil Webb (née Dendy) driving an Allis Chalmers high clearance row crow tractor, while moving implements up to Brighton Corporation land at Ditchling Beacon, which had been taken over by the Army. Sybil later worked as a Land Girl tractor driver for the National Institute of Agricultural Engineers both at Oxford and East Yorkshire, testing and developing lend-lease implements from America. She also helped with development work carried out on the Catchpole Sugar Beet Harvester.

Una Wilson (née Todd) with Standard Fordson tractor disc harrowing on Brighton Corporation land at Woodingdean near Falmer, Sussex. Una served as a tractor-driving instructor to other Land Girls at Brighton Racecourse.

Una Wilson (née Todd) collecting gorse for use at stack bottoms at Woodingdean, 1942. The tractor has pneumatic rear tyres as opposed to spade lug-iron wheels, which the girls called 'pueys'. The girl on the mudguard is Marie Saunders. The other girls are learning to drive tractors.

While working at F. & G. Mizzen Ltd at Woking, Surrey, Doris Kent ploughed with this International Pacemaker tractor. She competed in open ploughing matches against men, and won one prize for Best Maintained Tractor and Plough.

Drilling Oats at Streat, *c.* 1940. Helen Beard (née Coward) is sitting on a horse-drawn McCormick corn drill, converted for use behind a Fordson tractor. The tractor is driven by Sid Beard who later became her husband. Helen was known to all her colleagues as 'Johnny'.

Planting leeks at Ferring-on-Sea, 1943. Left to right: 'Joyce', Mollie Sivyer (née Cook), Lassie the dog, Beryl, a male fellow worker called 'Race', and Eric the tractor driver, who has his small son riding with him.

A Robot cabbage planter hitched behind a row crop tractor at F. & G. Mizzen Ltd's farm at Woking, Surrey. Doris Kent, smiling as usual, is on the right of the four Land Girls. The photograph was taken by Joy Deans (née Snow).

Two Land Girls with a tractor driver on a David Brown Cropmaster, near Thakeham, West Sussex. This tractor was unique and very popular because of its double seat; the extra seat enabled a driving instructor to sit next to the trainee driver, so keeping her under close supervision.

Linfield Nurseries at Thakeham, West Sussex, 1947. This is an Allis Chalmers row crop tractor, fitted with special wheels for use between very narrow rows of vegetable plants. Betty Merrett (née Long) has a cold job doing maintenance in the snow.

Betty Merrett (née Long), now in the sunshine, driving a Cletrac crawler tractor. Here at Linfield Nurseries, Thakeham, over 200 workers grew most varieties of vegetables. Betty was a tractor driver there for several years until 1947.

Laura Davitt (née Shepherd) driving a Caterpiller crawler tractor probably on a market garden at Walton-on-Thames, 1947. A number of these tractors were shipped over from America to help boost production of food on farms in England. More than one farmer lost his Caterpillar because the ship bringing it was sunk by enemy action.

Joy Deans (née Snow) driving a small crawler (make unknown) at Bonseys Farm, Woking. The implement attached (in transport position) is a steerage hoe, steered by an operator walking behind (see below).

'Charles and I with the "pram"'. Doreen Peskett (née Strange) driving with her future husband (they married in 1949), steering the hoe at Pound Cottage, Lynch Hill Farm, Burnham, Bucks, 1948.

# HAYMAKING

The tradition of women on farms being called upon to help with the haymaking was ages old. They had wielded pitchforks and hay rakes for generations to help dry the hay, wind-row it ready for collection and help with loading. Land Girls now came on to the farms and took this help many stages further, taking over the men's work of pitching up and loading hay wagons, pitching into the elevators and driving horses and tractors. As the girls became more experienced, some took on the more responsible jobs of mowing and turning hay with horses and tractors, and on several farms took over the very skilful task of building the towering haystacks.

The idyllic picture of a sun-bronzed pretty girl lifting a wisp of hay on a pitchfork was certainly attractive, but the girls soon found it wasn't quite like that. Long hours under a burning sun wielding a hayfork led to aching arms and legs accompanied by itching and often sunburn. Then there was the nightly ritual, while dog tired, of having to remove the hayseeds from socks and underclothes where they had become embedded.

There was compensation in having a feeling of great satisfaction, looking back at the clean hay fields and the gathered hay safely in the stacks, ensuring winter feed for all the animals.

East Sussex School of Agriculture trainee Land Girls – very much a posed picture for the benefit of the photographer. Note the smart uniform complete with ties.

Doreen Peskett (née Strange) building a load of hay at Mr Luckin's Warnham Court Farm, Horsham. The horse was called Boxer, and Mr Luckin is seen watching with his son Tommy.

Warnham Court Farm, Horsham, 1944. Doreen Peskett (née Strange) is driving a Standard Fordson tractor pushing a hay sweep. Notice the tractor had iron wheels, but the spade lugs have been removed to give a smoother ride on the hard ground.

East Sussex School of Agriculture, Plumpton, near Lewes, East Sussex. Land Girl trainee Joanne 'Merryweather' Matthewman, here raking hay, stayed on to work at the college. Joanne was born in India, and after her Land Army service went to Rhodesia, where she died in 1990.

Land Girls stacking hay on the Cowdray Estate at Midhurst, West Sussex. On the right is Betsy Sinclair (née Riddell).

Phyllis Dudgeon was very proud of this haystack she built at Newhouse Farm, Chiddingford, Surrey.

Betsy Sinclair (née Riddell) is on the left, haymaking at the Cowdray Estate near Midhurst.

Gladys Mount (née Yates) thatching a hayrick at Cheriton, Kent, 1944. Gladys had been taught to thatch by Herbert Mount, whom she married – but not until 1972, when he became a widower. She later became a Milk Marketing Board recorder, which she continued after 1950 as a civilian.

Trainee Land Girls at the Plumpton School loading hay trusses (that is, cut out of a haystack by hand). Almost 2,000 Land Girls passed through the school between July 1939 and 1944.

SEVEN

# HARVESTING & THRESHING

L and Girls wholeheartedly pitched in to the work of harvesting. The skills of 'shocking up' the sheaves of wheat, barley and oats, using a pitchfork to throw the sheaves up on to the wagons, and loading all came quickly, often as a form of self-preservation.

In the hand work of harvesting the girls learned that however hot the weather it was most unwise to bare one's arms and legs. The straw and the often encountered thistles in the sheaves could soon draw blood on bare skin. The itch caused by the barley 'oiks' penetrating the more tender parts could still be felt days later.

Girls were soon operating the self-binders that cut the corn, and often an all-girl team with a Land Army tractor driver was hard at work.

The long tiring hours of harvest would eventually come to an end, however delayed it might be by the weather, and a yard full of well-built corn ricks gave its own satisfaction.

The annual visit of the threshing tackle to each farm was a time when extra help was needed to cope with the dirty, dusty, monotonous tasks of feeding and clearing the machine. This was a job for which Land Girls were always used.

Kent War Agricultural Executive Committee was the first to decide that every travelling threshing machine would have its own permanent gang of Land Girls, usually four, to accompany the two men that maintained and ran the machine. Most of these gangs made up their rota so that each girl took a turn at the dustiest jobs. They all worked in the hope that the billet or hostel would be able to provide enough hot water for a bath at the end of the day; not always realized by any means.

'A better view of Helen' is recorded on the back of this photograph of Helen Beard (née Coward). This binder is driven by the tractor engine, and was an improvement on the previous type, designed for horses and driven by its own land wheel.

Hilda Chipp (née Howell) shocking (or stooking) sheaves of wheat in High Chivers field, at Lordington Farm, Rackton, West Sussex, 1944.

Eileen Mitchell (née Vile) stooking wheat sheaves at Pulborough, 1945. She remembers being 'fed up with stooking' when this photograph was taken. Like many other Land Girls, she soon found that stooking with bare legs produced painful sores.

Jose Rich raking corn stubbles with a horse rake at the East Sussex School of Agriculture. The horse, Captain, a Welsh Cob cross, is standing very much to attention as Jose holds him still. After the war Jose went to live in Canada.

Dorothy Jobson (née Eade) thatching a corn stack at Dedswell Farm, West Clandon, Surrey. Dorothy worked for Surrey WAEC and did thatching in season. She had been taught by her forewoman, who had been on a thatching course.

Thatching training at Clandon, Surrey, 1943. Placing the 'yelms' in the forked holder ready to be carried up the ladder is Kitty Brunton (née Chandler), and in the centre is Edna Mitchell.

Thatching training again at Clandon, near Guildford. Kitty Brunton (née Chandler) is on the ladder.

Herbert Mount stands proudly with his Women's Land Army thatching pupils in front of the stacks they have thatched, 1944. One of the pupils, later the wife of Mr Mount, was Gladys Yates.

Tom Bourn junior of Aldbourne, Sussex, was the threshing contractor for the East Sussex School of
Agriculture, where 200 to 250 acres of cereals were grown each year. Here trainee Land Girls are assisting
with sacking off the grain, and on the low corn stack (seen between the steam engine and threshing drum).
Wheat was put into 2¼ hundredweight sacks at that time – not easy to lift for loading on to wagons.

The unique Kent All-Girl Threshing Gang (also called the Golden Green Threshing Gang, named after
their base), seen at Horns Lodge, near Tonbridge, Kent, 3 March 1944. The six girls not only worked
on the machine, but operated the tractor and threshing drum, including moving it from farm to farm,
complete with a living van hitched behind the drum.

The Kent All-Girl Threshing Gang, March 1944. Back row, left to right: Stella Richardson, Betty Pearson, Nancy Johnson (née Jarvis), Doris Hawkins. Front row: Doris Dicker, Mrs Olive Bass (forewoman and driver). During the summer months the girls worked on Kent hop farms.

Four of the Kent threshing girls at work on the stack. Left to right: Stella Richardson, Doris Hawkins, Betty Pearson, and Nancy Johnson (née Jarvis).

The living van of the Kent threshing gang girls was only used for preparing meals. The girls lived in billets and cycled each day to the farm where they had left the machine. This scene was at Horns Lodge, Tonbridge, and the soldiers were in camp nearby. The van is marked up with the name, Arnold (Banbridges) Ltd – still existing today near Paddock Wood, and now steel fabricators.

The Kent threshing girls loading sacks of wheat on to a trailer. Nancy Johnson did admit that the loading was usually done by the men who collected it, but they were persuaded by the photographer to pose for this picture. The camera does not always tell the truth, it seems!

Women's Land Army threshing gang on Philip Westacott's Morants Court Farm, Dunton Green, Kent. The outfit belonged to Wellbands at Eynsford, Kent, and the feeder here is Tom. Notice that the steam engine, driven by Harry Baker, is parked opposite; having pulled the outfit to the farm, it was not used to drive the machine because of the wartime shortage of coal. The farm's own tractor was used to drive the belt, and its regular driver, George Campen, is sitting on it.

Land Girls feeding the threshing drum at Morants Court Farm. The field is called Hornbrook, and was rough steep chalkland, having only been ploughed up for extra wartime production. It only ever grew barley well, and was always plagued by rabbits from the surrounding woods.

Peggy Minor (née Bennison) served with a threshing gang at South Mimms in Hertfordshire, c. 1942. Here the girls pose by the tractor which is driving the belt to power the machine. 'Nelly' is on the left, Peggy Minor in the centre and above, and 'Milly' on the right.

Baling straw behind the threshing machine on an East Sussex War Agricultural Executive Committee farm near Peacehaven, 1948. Jean Stemp (née Ellis) worked on this machine.

# EIGHT

# OTHER JOBS

When male farm workers were leaving to join the Armed Forces in increasing numbers, the Land Girls were always there whatever job came up. With or without proper training, they soon became as skilled as the men, sometimes even better! 'The girls take advice more easily than men and are quick to grasp new ideas' was recorded at the time. They didn't always get the mucky jobs, but often did! Taking charge of poultry was a job at which Land Girls excelled, seeming to have the flair to persuade chickens to lay.

In the winter of 1942 as many as 200 of the 850 official pest controllers were Land Girls. This was a specialized job that usually meant rat catching. It was said that every rat on the farm cost 6s a year. The amount of food and animal feed eaten or spoiled by rats was estimated to amount to £25,000,000 a year. One girl later took charge of pest control over a large area of Hertfordshire.

A number of girls were attached to hospitals and military camps, to use vacant ground for production of vegetables and salad crops needed directly at these establishments. Land Girls were also employed at Kew Gardens, London, which fulfilled a wartime role of vegetable growing.

It would not be possible to list all the other jobs, but included is a selection: ditching, hedging, working in large dairies bottling and distributing milk (one girl delivered milk with a motor cycle and sidecar carrying a 17 gallon churn). One girl even became a water diviner.

A West Kent farmer reported: 'I have eleven Land Girls and would never have men again if I can help it. The women are cleaner, more conscientious and work far harder.' Overheard at a Wiltshire WLA rally was the comment: 'Tough? That girl is so tough she could use barbed wire as a chin strap!' Finally, as if their work as Land Girls wasn't sufficient, two East Kent girls joined the local Home Guard.

Land Girls filling and 'treading in' silage into a silo of the then popular type, made from wire mesh lined with heavy waterproof paper (known as Sisalcraft). The crop appears to be unchopped grass, heavy and tiring to fork. The photograph was produced by Lorna Newell, and probably comes from Leicester.

Land Girls filling a silo at the East Sussex School of Agriculture, *c.* 1940. This was the first silo at the college; it was sectional and made by Gascoignes, the early producers of milking machines. The material was lifted on to the trailer with a Wilder Cut-Lift. It was then loaded by hand into the silo. Helen Beard (née Coward) is seen in the centre with the fork.

Pest control instruction, Lewes Salvage Dump, Sussex, 1943. The rats were gassed using a powder which was ignited with a match, forcing fumes down into the rat holes. This salvage dump was infested with rats. The Land Girl on the left is Betty Merrett (née Long).

Land Girls trained as pest controllers setting rat traps, probably in Leicestershire. This photograph was produced by Lorna Newell, who completed the last of her ten-year service in the Land Army in the office of the County Secretary for Leicestershire.

Betty Merrett (née Long), furthest from the camera, setting rat bait in pig arks at a farm near Lewes, East Sussex, 1943.

Leicester Land Girls setting rat bait in a calf pen. The calf seems more interested in the camera. This photograph was taken by Lorna Newall.

Land Girls at the East Sussex School of Agriculture were not trained as blacksmiths, but were often sent to help Mr Smith when he needed assistance. Among other jobs they held horses being shod and pumped the bellows of the forge.

Peggy Few was one of twelve Land Girls sent to the Priestman factory at Hull to learn how to operate their excavators. Here she is in the cab of her Priestman excavator called The Cub, engaged on drainage work for the Thames Conservancy Board in the Thames Valley. The girls shovelling, Joyce Ebden (left) and Rosemary Herbert (right), were also excavator operators, photographed when they were all working on the same site, 13 January 1943.

Land Girls, including Marjorie Pither, working at a poultry breeding farm at Ditchling, East Sussex. Pedigree cockerels were reared and sent all over the country. Marjorie photographed her colleagues creosoting a poultry house to protect it.

A Land Girl job with a difference. Una Wilson (née Todd) became part of a Services Team to lead a National Savings drive at Chichester in late 1945. With both loudspeaker van and car, they toured the streets calling for volunteers as Savings Group Secretaries, and of course donations. Una rode in the van with the WRNS (Women's Royal Naval Service) girls, and they later toured Canterbury, then Durham and Northumberland. She is wearing non-issue made-to-measure breeches, which accounts for their smart cut.

# NINE

# MILKING & CATTLE

W omen have always excelled at milking (milkmaids of old) and calf-rearing, and Land Girls, with a little training and sometimes a lot of courage, were no exception. The Land Army years covered the transition of many farms from hand- to machine-milking. The girls' training mostly took account of hand-milking, but later machine-milking was taught. Of course any milker, man or woman, only became expert with practice on the job. It was recorded that one girl progressed from one cow per milking on her first day to thirteen cows by the end of the week.

There are many stories of dark, wet, cold mornings starting milking at 5 a.m., but the warmth of the cowshed and snuggling up to the cow's flanks while sitting on the milking stool did compensate. The possible exception was milking in the outdoor milking bail on high windswept downs in Wiltshire and elsewhere. Also recorded in detail are the 'kickers', cows that kicked the milker, knocked her off her stool, propelled the milking bucket across the shed, or merely put a dung-covered foot into it.

Land Girls were always good at calf-rearing, generally having more patience and kindness than male farm stockmen. Like most farm-workers, the girls could be divided into those who loved cattle and those who hated them.

The photographs produced seem to indicate a lively interest in bulls, not perhaps surprising with the many recorded incidents of the girls rescuing other farm-workers or fellow Land Girls from being hurt by angry bulls. A number of girls received awards for bravery while taking part in these rescues. In those days, pre-artificial insemination, bulls were kept on most farms, so the girls were in daily contact with these animals.

Land Girls were employed in the day-to-day feeding and care of fat and store cattle, but the number engaged in milking was by far the greater. Several score of girls ended their service in charge of milking herds, and few managed very large herds, including the breeding programmes.

East Sussex School of Agriculture Land Girl trainees learned milking on rubber cows. These devices evoke mixed memories, not all of them pleasant. An unkind instructor could fill the 'udder' with cold water, thus making the rubber teats stiffen. 'At least they didn't kick' was one comment.

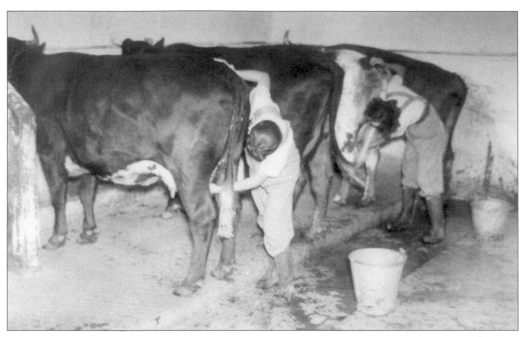

Cow stalls at the Plumpton Agriculture School. Here the girls are washing the cows' udders with warm water to clean them and stimulate the flow of milk, before starting hand-milking.

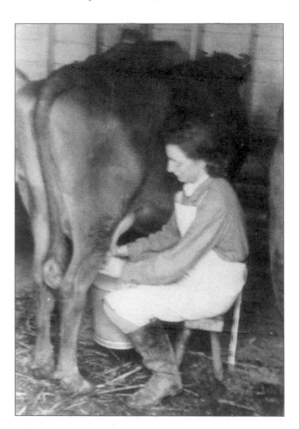

Doreen Rapley (née Crane) spent several years hand-milking at Mr Charles Shearing's farm at Southwater, Horsham, West Sussex. This photograph dates from 1941. Doreen served in the Land Army from July 1941 until it was disbanded in November 1950.

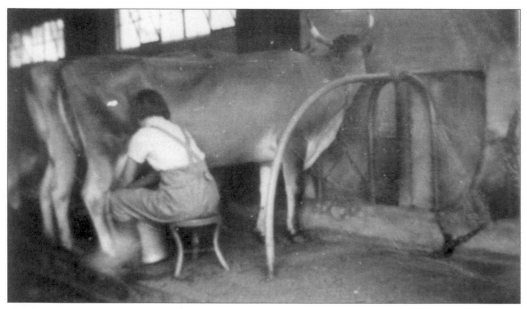

Gladys Mount (née Yates) milking a cow called Tattoo on Messrs Latter and Thompson's Newhouse Farm, Weald, near Sevenoaks, Kent, June 1940. Here seventy-five cows were milked daily using Land Army trainees. The girls were taught to milk by the cowmen, Jack Powell and Jack Hurley.

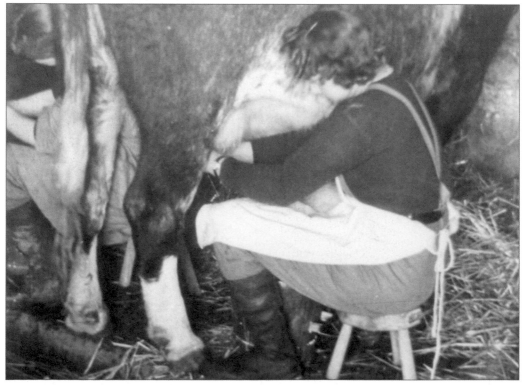

A trainee Land Girl milker at the East Sussex School of Agriculture at work on a Dairy Shorthorn, c. 1940.

Lola Cotton dressed in the 'Cover-knee Overalls' popular for milking at the time. It must have been a very progressive farm to be using a Gascoigne Miracle Bucket Milking Machine, a unit of which she is carrying. Two of these units worked off a vacuum pump with petrol engine, which could be wheeled up the shed behind the cows – once they had got used to the noise.

Gladys Mount (née Yates) working at
Newhouse Farm, Weald, Kent, on an early
milk carton filling machine, *c.* 1940.

Dorothy French (née Tattersall) with head cowman, Bill Buckwell, and Sue the pony at Mr John Harris'
Hackman's Farm, Plumpton, near Lewes, East Sussex, 1940. Dorothy delivered milk to all the houses
between the farm and Plumpton station, with the pony and milk cart, until the pony developed bad feet;
then she had to use a tradesman's bicycle which entailed several journeys.

A trainee Land Girl washing, most probably, udder cloths in an early washing machine at the Plumpton School of Agriculture.

Martha Smith (née Ferris) seen in 1942 feeding calves at the Horton Estate farm near Epsom in Surrey. This was a London County Council owned farm attached to five hospitals in the area. Martha tells me that the photo was taken by a press photographer who wanted an action picture at short notice, and in fact the bucket contained only water! The Land Girls on the estate normally wore ties when working, and she says she always looked as smart as this!

Mabel Gilbert (née Berry) at Prospect Farm, Havant, Hampshire, 1943. Mabel was a milker and was also responsible for taking calves to Havant market each week, driving a horse and cart with the calves tied up in the cart. She was billeted with the cowman in the village. The farm has now disappeared under the Leigh Park housing estate.

Barbara Greenshields (née Jupp). Barbara milked fourteen cows and reared all the heifer calves. Here she is feeding heifers at Sindles Farm, Westbourne, West Sussex, October 1946.

This photograph, taken on 18 January 1941, was used to illustrate an article, 'Back to the Land Girls!' in *Woman's Illustrated*. Ruby Johnson (née Caldbeck), one of the six Caldbeck sisters in the Land Army, is holding a bull on a pole at Earlye Farm, Wadhurst, East Sussex.

Yet another bull, Marmaduke, a pedigree Sussex. The photograph seems to imply that Phyllis Dudgeon doesn't really need a bull pole to keep him in order! Phyllis worked at Newhouse Farm, Shillinglee, Chiddingfold, Surrey, as a Land Girl from 1941 to 1950, then stayed on at the farm until 1959.

Friesian bull Fred is seen posing with Barbara Greenshields (née Jupp) at Sindles Farm, Westbourne, West Sussex, September 1944. Fred looks quite happy with the arrangement.

*T E N*

# HORSES

The older farm-workers, not needed in the armed forces, were often the horsemen, so there were considerably fewer Land Girl horsewomen than tractor drivers. These horsemen worked with a pair or team on ploughing and other cultivation jobs, but all farms had single horses used for odd jobs round the farm. Single horse work often came to the girls, and they took it up with enthusiasm. They became adept with a horse at general carting, including clamped roots for stock feed, hay, straw and manure. In so many ways a horse and cart are more manoeuvrable and versatile than a tractor and trailer, especially for one person feeding animals from a moving cart in the fields.

Many farms kept an odd lighter horse for jobs such as carting the daily churns of milk to the railway station, or collection point, delivering daily milk supplies to doorsteps in local towns and villages and the smaller local collections of supplies. This kind of work came readily to the girls, and when these light horses were also used for turning and tedding hay this too became one of their tasks.

During the later period of the war, when perhaps the older men retired and the girls became more experienced, many did take over the pairs of heavy work horses, with great success. A number of girls were able to compete in and sometimes win ploughing matches against strong male opposition in the horse classes.

The Land Girls who worked with the horses would surely all agree that you can get much fonder of a horse than a cow, pig or tractor, and that they made very pleasant companions through the days of working alone in distant fields.

A superb photograph of Thelma Wilkinson (née Walles) with a working heavy horse at the Leicestershire Co-operative Farms, Ansty, Elvington. Thelma distinguished herself by achieving 100 per cent in her Proficiency Test in Field Work. She served in the WLA from 1941 until 1945, when she had to leave after an accident.

Land Girl Lorna Newell (1940–50) ploughing with a pair of horses, Major and Blackbird, near Fontwell Magna in Dorset, 1944. Lorna was rearing calves, looking after breeding ewes and hand-milking. She was the only Land Girl on the farm. She completed her service working at the County WLA office in Leicester.

Plant Protection Ltd, Huntsfold, near Fernhurst, West Sussex, c. 1946. Ann Smeaton (right) works with a Suffolk Punch horse drilling small seeds with foreman, Bill Hunt. There were two Suffolk Punches in use at the farm.

Mary Hayes, a trainee Land Girl at the East Sussex School of Agriculture, Plumpton, with Boxer, harrowing an arable field. The school farmed about 800 acres during the war.

Another pupil Land Girl at the Plumpton School with Captain, *c*. 1940.

Doris Kent helping the carter, Mr Cresswell, to harvest sheaves at Dedswell Manor Farm, Clandon, Surrey, 1942. Doris was billeted with Mr and Mrs Creswell while working there.

This pony, called Nettle, and cart were used by the Land Girls on the Cowdray Estate at Midhurst, West Sussex, for all their odd jobs, including carting sugar beet and dung. Nettle was considered quiet enough for the girls to handle, but was remembered to have run off up the field a few times, when she felt like it. The Land Girl driving in the photograph is Gladys Billings.

Joan Shirt (née Robbins) and the potato planting gang, c. 1942. All the girls were employed by East Sussex War Agriculture Executive Committee. Joan was billeted at Pevensey, but the girls were working on Grant Curries Farm, Ovingdean, Brighton. Joan is on the extreme right. The girl wearing the overall jacket was 'Daisy', the ganger (that is, the forewoman).

'Me with Colonel', 1943. Colonel was over twenty years old, older in fact than young Barbara Greenshields (née Jupp). Barbara, working at Sindles Farm, Westbourne, West Sussex, is wearing her gaiters (made from her worn-out gum boots with the sole cut off) over her leather boots.

Gladys Marshall, a Land Girl farm trainee with Kitty, at Newhouse Farm, Shillinglee, Chiddingfold, Surrey, 1944. Kitty was well into her twenties at the time.

'Looking silly – Mollie, 1942.'
This was Mollie Sivyer (née Cook)
working on Mr Beale's market
garden at Ferring-on-Sea, West
Sussex. These were two horses hired
for the day at the market garden.
Mollie admits that really she was
'terrified of horses'.

Joan Mathewman working with Colonel at the East Sussex School of Agriculture at Plumpton. She stayed on at the school after training and later worked as a tractor driver, although she loved horses and Colonel was her favourite. Joan was well remembered because she often walked barefoot behind the horses when working.

Betty Bell (née Edelsten) on the right, sitting with fellow Land Girl Betty Norman on Starling at Plymtree, Devon, 12 January 1940. Betty Bell joined the Land Army in September 1939. These were early days and Betty Norman (a farmer's daughter who could milk before joining) had not yet received all her uniform.

# ELEVEN

# SHEEP & OTHER ANIMALS

The fact that most shepherds are men with years of specialized experience behind them is probably the reason why very few girls became shepherdesses. It is possible too that a farmer could have such an important employee registered as working in a reserved occupation, and thus exempted from being called up. However, one Land Girl was commended later in the war for being in sole charge of a flock in North Wales for over four years.

A large number of girls were employed at busy times of sheep husbandry. Helping with sheep-dipping and the annual shearing were common. Girls also soon acquired skills in dagging in the dangerous fly strike periods, and trimming hoofs. In August 1945 two girls working in Devon won a sheep-shearing class in a competition at Morehampstead.

An enormous number of girls found that their day-to-day duties included seeing to the pigs, from the odd pig kept to provide bacon to quite large herds either housed or kept in the open. A girl recorded that she spent her days with a light horse and cart carrying feed out to the pigs and poultry kept in arks across the open fields. The horse was also used to pull the arks to fresh ground each day. Many Land Girls found that pigs can be very pleasant and clean animals when given the chance.

Most of the girls on smaller farms found themselves feeding the chickens morning and evening and being responsible for shutting them in safely at night. They worked too in more intensive egg production units, and girls were reported as working at the intensive rearing of rabbits for food.

One caring girl was released from Land Army duties to become a full-time assistant to a veterinary surgeon, having discovered an intense interest in animal welfare.

The East Sussex School of Agriculture Land Girl pupils move sheep with Fred Pick, the shepherd. He taught some of his shepherding skills. The sheep are Southdowns, one of the breeds kept at the school.

Helen Beard (née Coward) holding a lamb on a rare day off, spent visiting the sheep at the nearby Stanmer Park, Brighton. Helen was both student and instructor at the East Sussex School of Agriculture from 1939 until 1944.

Betsy Sinclair (née Riddell) on the left and Gladys Billings working with the shepherd at the Cowdray Estate, Midhurst, West Sussex, spring 1940.

Betty Bell (née Edelsten) reared twenty-four lambs on the bottle in 1940 (a bad year when many ewes died) while working on Mr Sumtion's farm at Plymtree, Devon. Mr Sumtion was a member of the strict Plymouth Brethren. He and his family were not permitted to work on Sundays, so the Land Girls did it all instead.

Land Girls dipping sheep in Sussex, possibly at the East Sussex School of Agriculture at Plumpton.

An East Sussex School of Agriculture trainee Land Girl hand-clipping a Kerry ewe. There was a small flock of Kerry sheep at the school.

Helen Beard winding the fleece of a Border/ Leicester ewe in Moat Yard at Plumpton. Helen remembers the lovely feeling of the lanolin from the wool on her arms after fleece-winding which entailed rolling the fleece into as small a bundle as possible with the clipped wool outwards, then making a rope of wool to tie the bundle tight.

A Large White sow and piglets in Ox Pasture at the East Sussex School of Agriculture. It was unusual to tether a pig, and the sow's nose was ringed to prevent it from digging up the pasture. Trainee Land Girls looked after and learned about pigs as part of their general Farm Work course.

Daphne Turner (née Hudson) feeding some rare ginger-brown Tamworth pigs. She was working at Wetherhill Farm, Icklingham, Bury St Edmunds, Suffolk. Feed was very short at this time.

Mr Sumtion's farm at Plymtree, Devon, 1939. Betty Bell is caring for newly hatched chicks.

Betty Hall (née Edelsten) feeding hens at Plymtree, Devon, early 1940. After working in Gloucestershire, Betty moved in 1944 to take charge of 200 pigs being fattened in Bermondsey, South London. The pigs were kept on an old council dump off the Walworth Road and beside the River Thames. They belonged to a Mr Vicimi, a young man waiting to be called up into the RAF. He collected Betty each day from her billet on the back of his motor cycle and returned her after work.

Audrey Taplin and her dog feed poultry at Ditchling in East Sussex. This farm specialized in breeding pedigree cockerels, which were sent all over the country.

Hilda Howell (née Chipp) manages to recruit a new 'Land Girl' – perhaps a dog with a name like Tinker was not ideal Land Army material. Hilda worked with Barbara Greenshields (née Jupp) at Sindles Farm, Westbourne, West Sussex.

# TWELVE

# THE TIMBER CORPS

The Timber Corps was a separate part of the Women's Land Army formed in April 1942, and the girls wore their own distinctive green beret with a unique badge. By the time it was disbanded on 3 April 1946 over 6,000 girls had worked hard in forests and timber mills. They not only had to replace the men now serving in the Armed Forces, but had to cope with all the extra timber needed for the war effort. Production of wooden pit props for the coal mines was always an important role, but there were also special needs such as wood to build the Mosquito aircraft, wood-based mine-sweeper ships, and even alder wood used in the production of special charcoal for high explosives.

Whereas Land Girls were employed directly by their farmer employers, the Timber Corps girls were employed by the Ministry of Supply; their pay, accommodation, health care and welfare were the responsibility of the Home Timber Production Department.

Girls were subject to a second more stringent medical examination before acceptance into the Corps, and were then sent for four weeks' training. During this time they were assessed, and then offered work in one of four main departments.

Measuring involved estimating timber, standing, felled and sawn. Often these girls also took over what was previously the foreman's work, relating to production returns, pay sheets for workers, and income tax records. An early Timber Corps job was for a large number of measurers, who were given the task of visiting all the medium to large stands of timber in the country to assess the country's stocks of various types of trees. This very arduous and difficult job was completed in good time.

Saw-milling women took over the all-male preserve of operating huge saws, and other heavy work. By the end of the war many Timber Corps girls were foremen and managers of saw-mills, in charge of many other female and male employees.

Haulage and transport were important, and involved loading and driving timber lorries and tractors, both in the woods and to the mills. Girls in Scotland used horses to extract timber most successfully.

In forestry work the jobs were divided between felling of trees, trimming off the tree trunks, cross-cutting timber into required lengths and clearing the discarded twigs and branches after the timber was removed.

A review of the health of Timber Corps girls made in 1945 revealed above average health and weight. The most widespread serious ailment found was rheumatism, no doubt caused by exposure to the elements in all weathers, and a general lack of adequate drying facilities for work clothes. It was not unknown for the girls living in the forest camps to have to dress each morning in the still damp clothes of the previous day.

Women's Timber Corps girls arriving for work at Priory Hill, Cambridge, 1943. There they were engaged in thinning and felling larch. The girls were in billets at St Neots and Caxton, found for them by Cambridge Ministry of Supply who supplied cycles to get them to work. The photograph was taken by Jean Heggs (née Hunt).

Winnie Catterell from Wigan started work at
Southwater, Horsham, Sussex, as a 'feller' then
went on to become a 'measurer'. A measurer
was responsible for calculating the volume
of timber that was being felled, sawn, etc.
This figure was used to record the amount
of timber passing through their hands, and to
calculate the workers' wages.

'Jean' from Nottingham working
at Cottesbrooke, Gilsborough,
Northamptonshire, 1943. Jean was a feller;
they were entitled to wear a distinctive brass
Crossed Axes badge on their armband.

Another Timber Corps scene at Cottesbrooke. 'Jean' and 'Betty', who comprised Jean Heggs' (née Hunt) gang, pose while sawing a tree down. Jean points out, however, that they have forgotten to cut the sawing wedge out with an axe first.

Cross-cutting a log at Thornbury, Holesworthy, Devon, 1942. 'Haze', aged twenty, is on the left, and Eileen Orchard (née Shore), aged eighteen, is on the right.

Girls from the Women's Timber Corps
levering logs into position with a cant hook
at Priory Hill, Cambridge, 1942.

Resting on a lorry, Cottesbrooke, Northamptonshire, 1943. 'Jean' and 'Betty' are at the back, while Ida
Chandler is at the front on the left, and on the right is a girl who left to marry an American airman. They
loaded logs, took them to the station, and then unloaded them on to railway wagons. A Timber Corps
lorry driver was killed when the brakes failed while carrying timber.

Highmeadow Sawmills in the Forest of Dean, August 1944. Left to right: 'Jean', 'Peggy', 'Mary', 'Eileen', and Sheila McIntyre (née Meredith). All the girls were measurers except Peggy, who was a sawyer.

The girls working at Bishop's Wood, Shropshire, take a chance to relax in the sun, 1943. Hilda Pearson (née Roylands), who transferred from the Women's Land Army, stands on the right at the back. To the left of her is Cecily Turner. The two blond girls are sisters and had both been hairdressers in civilian life. (See also page 106.)

A Women's Timber Corps group at Oundle, Northamptonshire, 1944. Jean Heggs (née Hunt) is now forewoman and is on the extreme right of the middle row. The ganger 'Ivy' is the bigger girl in the centre.

Tom, one of the Irish woodsmen who came over to help wartime timber production, sits between 'Irene' (on the left with axe) and 'Jean' (with billhook), who both came from the north of England. The photograph was taken at Eltisley, Cambridgeshire, in 1942.

Timber Corps girls on a very special job, 'making blancmange', at Bishop's Wood, Shropshire, June 1942. The two blonde girls are sisters, and the girl behind is Cecily Turner. The photograph was taken by Hilda Pearson (née Roylands).

*THIRTEEN*

# SOCIAL EVENTS

Some of the luckier girls enjoyed invitations to the dances at Army and Royal Air Force camps, and later the American Air Force bases, which did much to boost morale in both directions. However, many Land Girls found themselves billeted in remote villages and farmsteads well beyond reasonable cycling distance, or convenient bus routes, to the nearest towns. Some city-born girls found it impossible to adapt to the country, but, faced with little alternative, most coped.

The better local representatives did their best to bring isolated girls together, often in their own houses, at tea parties and evening meals. Sometimes they offered their own bathrooms and plenty of hot water for girls who lacked these basic facilities at their billets.

Those grouped together at the hostels fared better, with occasional organized transport (albeit often in lorries) to town on Saturday nights. The girls organized their own home-made entertainments and competitions at the hostels, and many happy hours were enjoyed. Some girls based near country towns formed their own WLA Clubs, and met regularly for entertainment and social evenings in available premises.

Those who adapted well to rural life found themselves involved in local organizations, varying from the church choir, the local Young Farmers Club (the YFCs made special efforts to recruit Land Girls), to many a local pub darts and shove-halfpenny team. The girls were not above forming their own football and cricket teams and competing with the men.

As the war years progressed a number of girls formed attachments to local young men, and servicemen, so that weddings with Land Army guards-of-honour, wielding pitchforks and hoes, were the order of the day.

Horsham WLA Club Cricket Team, 1943. Back row, second from the left, is Rosalind Cox, captain. She was the sister of George Cox, a well-known Sussex County cricketer at the time. Front row, second from the right, is Muriel Bushby (née Merrett). On the extreme right is Elsie Bailey. They played for two seasons, against such teams as Army Ladies and local General Post Office teams. The only match that Muriel remembers winning was on 2 July 1942, when they beat the ATS (Auxiliary Territorial Service, i.e. Women's Army) 94 runs to 50, at the County Cricket ground at Horsham.

Land Army 'Ladies Football Fun Team', 1944. These were girls working for the Surrey War Agriculture Executive Committee based at Burchett's Farm. The shirts were borrowed from Queen's Regiment barracks at Stoughton, near Guildford. They played against another ladies' team; the result has been forgotten. Back row, third from the right, is Kitty Brunton (née Chandler), and third from the left is Enid Mitchell.

A Land Girl Football Team from a hostel at Torrington, Devon, who called themselves Land Army Rangers, 1948. They played a team of local men called Non-such Wanderers. The men had to run with one arm behind their backs, but in spite of training hard with the boys from a school opposite their hostel, the Land Army Rangers still lost 7–0. Jean Stemp (née Ellis) is on the left of the back row, and next to her is Jean Quan. Some of the shorts bear a striking resemblance to cut-off Land Army breeches!

The Verdley Revue performed at Plant Protection Ltd, Hurstfold, Fernhurst, West Sussex, c. 1947. Left to right: Geoff Bacon, Dorothy Lockie, Mary Wright, Gordon Wright. The male 'Land Girls' seem to be the most vigorous workers!

A most professional-looking production by Midhurst WLA Club of *Cinderella*, *c.* 1944. Back row, left to right: Barbara Stapely, Diana Woods, Gladys Billings, Hazel Tracey, Rosanna ?, Nancy Stocks (née Smith), Ivy Edwards, Grace Glue (née Kirk), 'Abbe'. Front row: Betsy Sinclair (née Riddell), Elizabeth ?.

A Wild West Show by the Land Girls at Forest House Hostel, Mannings Heath, Horsham, West Sussex. The photograph was provided by Inez Kensett (née Rapley), who is in there somewhere.

A Land Army wedding at Streatham, south-east London, 1945. The bride was Brenda Bissenden who with her 'Guard Of Honour' came from the Hatchetts Hostel at Newdigate, Surrey and was a trained thatcher. The bridegroom's name is not remembered. Jean Morris (née Monk) was a guest inside the church.

A Land Army wedding at Torrington, Devon, 1948. The bride was Ann Harvey who married a Mr Hutchins. The photograph was taken by a local photographer, Fred Woodward, and was produced by Jean Stemp (née Ellis) who is among the pitchforks of the 'Guard of Honour'.

Another Land Army wedding as Helen Beard (née Coward) marries Sid, a fellow instructor at the East Sussex School of Agriculture at Plumpton, 10 September 1942. The 'Guard of Honour' was provided by her colleagues and pupils holding pitchforks and rakes.

Sid and Helen Beard walk from St Michael's Church, Plumpton, to the reception at the school, followed by their guests in uniform. No wedding cars were available in these wartime conditions.

A WLA Rally at Oaklands Park, Chichester, September 1947. These bachelor young farmer judges are very seriously deciding the winner of the Best Ankle Competition. Muriel Bushby (née Merrett) is third from the right in the line-up. The name of the winner has been lost in the mists of time.

Land Girls give a hand to the band at a WLA rally at Mote Park, Maidstone, 1943. Pat Ware (née Taylor) is learning to play the xylophone.

A coach outing to the seaside for the Land Girls of Westfield House Hostel at Fontwell, near Chichester, West Sussex, 1949.

Three thirsty Land Girls snatch a quick half pint at the side of the Plough Inn (believed to be at Plummers Plain, near Horsham, West Sussex). On the right is Jean Holford, and in the middle is a girl known as 'Copper Knob'.

# FOURTEEN

# RALLIES & PARADES

Rallies and parades held throughout the war years were considered essential for morale and recruitment. King George VI and Queen Elizabeth both took a great interest in the Land Girls, and attended a number of parades, including several at Buckingham Palace. The rallies were held all over the country, and employers were asked to release their girls to attend. Public and notable local figures would attend the occasion and make encouraging speeches. Often the rallies were used for presentations of proficiency certificates and badges, new long service armbands, and the half diamonds for sewing on to them for each six months service.

The vexed question of how the girls re-shaped their hats led to many admonitions and the issue of instructional leaflets. At a rally at Aylesbury the then Minister of Food, Lord Woolton, remarked: 'Why do some of them wear different hats from the others?' The County Chairman had to reply: 'It's all the same hat, but they wear it differently!' It is possible this incident and others led to the issue of berets before some of the parades held in London, the offending hats being banned from use during the parade.

The Land Army continued until its final disbandment in 1950, when numerous parades were held in every county and in London at Westminster Abbey.

Worthing 'Wings for Victory' Parade, when the Land Girls joined the other services on the Sea Front, 1943. Worthing WLA Club organized this group. The machine behind them appears to be an American lend-lease Peg Drum threshing machine. Mollie Sivyer (née Cook) stands behind the left banner holder.

Four Land Girls promote National Savings Certificates, Lee-on-Solent, early 1940s. The occasion is not known, but the photograph was provided by Daphne Turner (née Hudson).

Land Girls' rally at Arundel Castle, probably on 9 May 1943. The girls nearest the camera are wearing berets, which indicate they were members of the Women's Timber Corps, allied to the Land Army.

These West Sussex Land Girls formed up at Arundel Castle and then paraded through the town, 9 May 1943. The girl holding the Chichester District board was known as 'Johnny'. They were preceded by a military band.

West Sussex Land Army Rally, when 700 Land Girls from the county met at Arundel Castle, 9 May 1943. The castle was the residence of the Duke of Norfolk, then Joint Parliamentary Secretary to the Minister for Agriculture. The speaker is Betsy Sinclair (née Riddell) who coined the sentence 'We may not be glamorous but we are vital' in her speech. On the platform are the Duke and Duchess of Norfolk, with their children, Lady Mary (left) and Lady Anne (right) and their dog.

The unmistakable figure and hat of Lady Trudie Denman, Honorary Director of the Women's Land Army, making a presentation. The venue is somewhere in West Sussex.

A WLA rally at Wiston, the home of Sir Walter and Lady Burrell, 1946. At the microphone is Jack Warner, well-known radio and film personality at that time. His popular offerings included monologues about people's jobs, and specially for this occasion he produced one about 'The lifter-uppers of cow's tails'. Left to right: John Goring, Sir Walter Burrell, Miss Forbes-Adams (County WLA Secretary), Lady Burrell (West Sussex Women's Land Army Chairman) and Lady North.

Land Girls are just coming from Church Parade at Bedhampton Church, Havant, Hampshire, 1943. The girl on the left of the front row is Doris Godwin, and on the right is Wanda, a naval officer's daughter. At their side was the girls' local representative, Miss Walmer White, who was responsible for the welfare of Land Girls in an area from Havant to Rowlands Castle. She was very popular and is remembered with affection. Mabel Gilbert (née Berry), who provided the photograph, is one of the girls whose faces can be seen at the back.

West Sussex Women's Land Army Final Rally, at Bishop Otter College, Chichester, West Sussex, 16 September 1950. Second from the left in front is the Hon. Mrs Walter Burrell (Chairman of West Sussex WLA Committee). Third from the left is Miss Forbes-Adams, the popular WLA County Secretary.

The first London Lord Mayor's Show after the Second World War, 9 November 1946. (Notice the empty bomb-sites behind.) Among the marching Land Girls are Connie Edwards (née Caldbeck), third marcher back on the left-hand side, and one of her sisters, Christabel, the last marcher in the right-hand column.

Doreen Rapley (née Crane) was one of the West Sussex Land Girls chosen to parade in front of Queen Elizabeth at Buckingham Palace to mark the disbanding of the Land Army, 21 October 1950. An interesting note is that just before the parade the girls were issued with green berets to wear instead of the famous 'pork pie' hats. We suspect the reason was the weird and wonderful shapes into which these long-serving Land Girls had managed to contort their hats.

The scene in the inner courtyard of Buckingham Palace, as the Queen makes her final inspection, 21 October 1950.

Queen Elizabeth pauses to talk to a Land Girl. Notice the parts of their armbands that indicate at least eight years' service.

Representatives of the Women's Land Army attend the National Harvest Thanksgiving Service at Westminster Abbey, attended by His Majesty King George VI and the Queen, Saturday 30 October 1948. Phyllis Dudgeon was one chosen to represent West Sussex WLA in the Guard Of Honour. She was in the right-hand line of girls just out of view. Notice that the green berets were again used at this parade. Those famous hats had a lot to answer for.

# CONCLUSION

The number of Land Girls on the farms of England, Wales and Scotland swelled from 7,445 in November 1940 to 76,961 in August 1943, when recruiting ceased for a time because of a greater need of women in munition factories. Although there was no need to increase the Land Army's numbers after this date, recruiting was resumed to replace those lost to the service. The last figure available was 25,674 in March 1947. However, one girl in West Sussex joined as late as 1949, and served only the one year before disbandment in October 1950.

The Land Girls were denied many of the privileges of the Armed Forces during the war, and there was much dissatisfaction in 1945 when it was realized that released Land Girls were to receive no monetary gratuity or de-mob clothing, as were members of the other services. Winston Churchill was deaf to pleas on their behalf, and Lady Trudi Denman, still Honorary Director, was so incensed that she resigned in protest in March 1945, but all to no avail. The only concession made was permission to keep their overcoat, socks and shoes when released. Many girls felt very strongly that they were only offered 'gratitude, but no gratuity', having done so much in the service of their country.

It is very sad that the official Land Army records were (inadvertently?) destroyed soon after the war, and what records exist now are extremely slender. We have, for example, knowledge of only one lady who holds the coveted gold ten year badge, and it would be thrilling to know the total number presented.

Both of us have been privileged to meet and spent time with so many wonderful ladies, who have given us their time freely and allowed us to copy and use their treasured photographs.

We are both very conscious that we never met what could be a large number of ex-Land Girls who did not enjoy the period of their service, and so did not answer our plea for help. However, almost all of the ladies we did meet have said, in various ways, 'Our Land Army days were some of the best years of our lives.' What more is there to say?

## WOMEN'S LAND ARMY (ENGLAND AND WALES).
# RELEASE CERTIFICATE.

The Women's Land Army for England and Wales acknowledges

with appreciation the services given by

**Miss D.M.Kent,**                    **W.L.A.71077.**

who has been an enrolled member for the period from

**28th. March,**          1942 to   **10th. January,**   1946

and has this day been granted a willing release.

Date **10th. January, 1946.**

COUNTY SECRETARY, WOMEN'S LAND ARMY.

Doris Kent's WLA Release Certificate, issued in 1946.

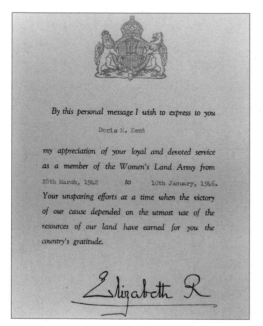

*By this personal message I wish to express to you*

Doris M. Kent

*my appreciation of your loyal and devoted service*
*as a member of the Women's Land Army from*
28th March, 1942          to          10th January, 1946.
*Your unsparing efforts at a time when the victory*
*of our cause depended on the utmost use of the*
*resources of our land have earned for you the*
*country's gratitude.*

*Elizabeth R*

Her Majesty Queen Elizabeth's Thank You message
given to all Land Girls leaving after the war.

NORTHAMPTONSHIRE INSTITUTE OF AGRICULTURE
1945-46

Northampton Institute of Agriculture ran a postwar course (as did Cambridge) for all servicemen and women who wished to become employed in agriculture after their release. The course lasted for thirty-one weeks.

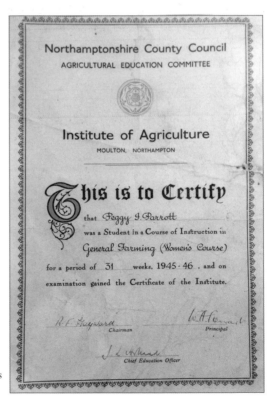

Peggy Parrott attended this course and received this certificate for completing it.

A final gesture: 'The Gratuity Snap' – Ann Mellor (left), who left the Land Army to join the police force, and Muriel Carter (right). Land Girls were allowed to retain only their greatcoats, shoes and socks on being released. Ann and Muriel demonstrate the way they felt about this derisory concession.

# ACKNOWLEDGEMENTS

We would like to thank very sincerely the many people who helped with the preparation of this book, most especially those ex-Women's Land Army ladies who so willingly lent us their photographs to copy and gave so much of their time to helping with and verifying the caption information.

We must also acknowledge our thanks to the Weald & Downland Open Air Museum, whose Women's Land Army exhibition to mark fifty years from the end of the Second World War brought to our notice the wealth of previously unpublished photographs.

Should we have unknowingly infringed the copyright of any photograph used in this book, we apologize most sincerely, and upon notification will ensure that any future edition will contain full acknowledgement.

# BIBLIOGRAPHY

**Non-Fiction**

Barraud, E.M. (1946) *Set My Hand Upon The Plough*, Worcester, Littlebury.

———— (1948) *Tail Corn*, London, Chapman & Hall.

Cowley, Irene (1985) *Over My Shoulder*, Ilfracombe, Stockwell.

Gangulee, Professor N. (1943) *The Battle of The Land*, London, Lindsay Drummond.

Geere, Marjorie (1987) *Reminiscences Of A Land Girl In Witham*, Witham, Poulter.

Grayson, Peggy (1994) *Buttercup Jill*, Ipswich, Farming Press.

Green, Michael & Dunbar, Evelyn (1942) *A Book of Farmcraft*, London, Longman.

Hall, Anne (1993) *Land Girl*, Bradford-Upon-Avon, Ex Libris Press.

Huxley, Gervas (1962) *Lady Denman G.B.E.*, London, Chatto & Windus.

Hyndham, Oonagh (1990) *Wartime Kent 1939–1945*, Rainham, Meresborough Books.

Iddon, Jean (1947) *Fragrant Earth*, London, Epworth Press.

Joseph, Shirley (1946) *If Their Mothers Only Knew*, London, Faber & Faber.

Joyce, Knighton (1994) *Land Army Days – Cinderellas Of The Soil*, Bolton, Aurora.

Knappett, Rachel (1946) *Pullet On The Midden*, London, Michael Joseph.

———— (1953) *Wait Now*, London, Country Book Club.

Mant, Joan (1994) *All Muck, No Medals*, Lewes, Book Guild.

Meiggs, Russell (1949) *Home Timber Production 1939–1945*, London, Crosby Lockwood.

Mist, Ellen (1992) *Aw-Ahhr! Experiences In The Women's Land Army*, Penzance, United Writers.

Nelson, G.K. (1992) *Countrywomen On The Land*, Stroud, Sutton.

Sackville-West V. (1944) *The Women's Land Army*, London, Michael Joseph.

Tillet, Iris (1988) *The Cinderella Army*, London, Michael Joseph.

Timber Corps Members (c. 1945) *Meet The Members*, Bristol, Bennett Bros.

Turner, Norah (1992) *In Baggy Brown Breeches And A Cowboy Hat*, Rainham, Meresborough Books.

Twinch, Carol (1990) *Women On The Land*, Cambridge, Lutterworth Press.

Wells, Irene (1984) *My Life In The Land Army*, Alcester, Williams.

Whitton, Barbara (1953) *Green Hands*, London, Faber & Faber.

Wilding, Frances (1972) *Land Girl At Large*, London, Paul Elek.

Williams, Mavis (1994) *Lumber Jill: Timber Corps*, Bradford-Upon-Avon, Ex Libris Press.

Williams, Irene (1993) *Life After The Land Army*, Alcester, Williams.

**Fiction**

Huth, Angela (1994) *Land Girls*, London, BCA.